ENGLISH

JEET THAYIL

PENGUIN

An imprint of Penguin Random House

HAMISH HAMILTON

USA | Canada | UK | Ireland | Australia
New Zealand | India | South Africa | China

Hamish Hamilton is part of the Penguin Random House group of companies
whose addresses can be found at global.penguinrandomhouse.com

Published by Penguin Random House India Pvt. Ltd
4th Floor, Capital Tower 1, MG Road,
Gurugram 122 002, Haryana, India

First published by Penguin India 2003

This edition published in Hamish Hamilton by Penguin Random House India 2022

Copyright © Jeet Thayil 2022

ISBN 9780670097531

Typeset in Adobe Garamond Pro by Manipal Technologies Limited, Manipal
Printed at Replika Press Pvt. Ltd, India

www.penguin.co.in

Shakti, Shakti, Shakti

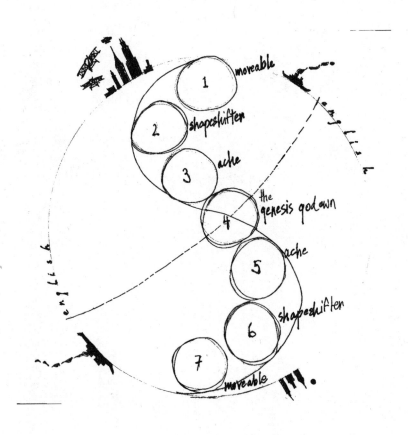

1 moveable
2 shapeshifter
3 ache
4 the genesis godown
5 ache
6 shapeshifter
7 moveable

english

CONTENTS

IV. THE GENESIS GODOWN

V. ACHE

VI. SHAPESHIFTER

VII. MOVEABLE

AUTHOR'S NOTE

English originally appeared in 2003, a co-publication by Penguin India and Rattapallax Press, New York. It has been in print ever since. For its reappearance in this two-in-one edition, I'd like to thank Aparna Kumar, whose vision steered the book. The lines in italics in 'English' quote the gospel according to Thomas, from the Gnostic Papyri in the Coptic Museum at Old Cairo, Vol I. (Cairo, 1956), p. 89, line 10 to p. 99, line 28. The Gnostic library—13 volumes found in 1945 in Nag Hamadi, Upper Egypt—most likely dates from the fourth century AD. 'He Do the Husband' takes its title from a section of T.S. Eliot's original manuscript for *The Waste Land*. Ezra Pound deleted the passage and it was never subsequently used. The lines in italics in 'About the Author' quote from Gerald Stern's 'Hot Dog', from *Odd Mercy* (by permission of W.W. Norton & Co.) There is a reference to Gerald (Stern) in the poem's last stanza; it refers also to Nissim (Ezekiel) and Dom (Moraes); T.J.S. (George) is my father. The drawing on page vii, a representation of the book's in-seven structure, is modelled after Robert Wilson's seven-act play, *Stalin*. Parts 1 and 7, 2 and 6, 3 and 5 reflect each other; part 4 is the point of reflection. My thanks to the New York Foundation for the Arts for a 2003 Poetry Fellowship that helped me to make this book. As ever, the collection would not have been possible without its tripartite *deus ex libris*—T.J.S. George, Ammu George and Sheba Thayil.

I

MOVEABLE

ABOUT THE AUTHOR

Born in a hamlet near the southern Him-
alayas, the author's youth was spent in,
and under, the twin shadows of madness
and avalanche. "Of the two, loony tunes
are much more better," he was told by
his long-suffering Ma, who, ten months
pregnant ("he was not wanting to come out,
poor baba"), married her father's long-lost
brother. Born on honeymoon, the author's
his mother's first cousin, his father's great
nephew, and his step-sister's loving, ah,
husband, though that comes a little later.
Right about now it's time to switch view-
points to the man of the mommy himself.

Title for an imaginary sequel:
Ishmael, Fishmeal, call me what you want,
just call me, okay? Stop. Go syllabics:
One only I recall of all the fish-
like faces of my wives, oh, one. I swear
now, on the moment's talk I am allowed,
swear her hair and every pore was adored
by light. I'd wake to the smell of guavas
poached in milk, the sound of peacocks adance
in dawn-soaked hanging gardens, and she, a
season with wings. Not the youngest, the most
beautiful, or the most fertile, but she
is the one I remember now, countries

away from the plangent peril of Hind,
the rainy country I was king of, once.
I don't ask for much. Keep your silver,
give me instead something simple, a field
of blue, say, or green, or a square foot of
red, the colour bleeding at the edges,
held together by happenstance and pins,
and let the good owl Severn be my guide.
He, no I, was walking in Colaba,
on a day late in the monsoon, looking
for *The Times of Bombay-not-Mumbai* and
a smoke of O and the next thing we know
I'm standing on Sixth, watching ruin, with
a handful of rain and a prophecy,
no idea in my head what next to do,
say, be, or think, or any thing, except

the taste of ash in the pulverized air,
this morning by the Flatiron, drifting up-
town, just before the savage winter of
2001, everything settled
at last, the star anise folded between
my eyes saying, I am not of your race.

Truth is for years I suffered whenever
I ate, my father told me as I stepped
into this weird new world, *pork, not bacon*
but pork, and he nodded at the baby
back ribs and vindaloo-rice on my plate.
"But dad," I said, "but Nissim, but Dom, but
T.J.S., how will I walk in the world

and not eat of its food? How will I walk?"
I asked my sweet old father, asking him
to help me with this last thing, this last time.
*You keep / kosher to show your love for the
void*, Gerald replied. I knew he meant *word*,
love for the word, is what he meant, I know.
The author now lives in New York City.

MOVEABLE

Alright, I admit it, I am struggling, I am.
Naming the sacred is not a job you take
lightly, not, that is, if you want to live
to any half-ripe sort of age. Until 1989
we were frequent companions. I visited
you, entertained you—in Bombay behind
the Byculla zoo—and, merely a month later,
in HK, we lived in Repulse Bay on a junk.
After that my memory becomes hazier
with pain. Was it you I spent a month with
in Chiang Mai, smoking opium in a stilt-
house with the chief and his daughters?
We had so much money then, it was as if
we were on vacation from real life forever.
I remember: I am bringing home goodies
—imported coffee, cigarettes, geraniums
in a jar. I am sitting on a scooter,
you are in the sidecar, laughing in tongues.
Who would have guessed the disaster
in store, or how rarely you would appear
in the decade of denial? I am in my thirties,
shirtless, a baby elephant's head grows
out of my shoulders, I carry a beer-
belly and shades. My mother is bathing.
I am on guard duty, which I enjoy.
As my Asiatic time came to a close
you and I grew reckless, racing borrowed
toys through the streets of ghost towns

patrolled by soldiers, priests, guard dogs,
and always the inscrutable face and
lotus feet of the first godman, Sri Sri
Baba Ba. On the airplane we sat
by the aisle—sharing drinks, magazines,
maps to the world—measuring our journey
in statute miles. At JFK you scurried
off for coffee. "Back in a mo," you said,
"and remember, yaar, the nail in your head
is moveable. So move it why don't you?"
In the fall of 2001, I do, I walk
from Roosevelt Station to a basement room
in Jackson Heights, past Hindi movie houses,
cut-rate travel agents, kabab halls, suit-
sari shops, paan-DVD parlours, psychics.
You, I am beginning to suspect, are not here.

SKEWED

I am on a street, already *somewhere*—
say downtown, say Perry and Hudson,
where Hart Crane lived for a summer
and Dylan Thomas fell, as if into sleep.
I am poor. I am no tourist. I am hitching
my cargos past the angular bones in my hip.
I wear a black-and-white scarf at my throat,
folded not knotted, my coat buttoned up,
and I know I am ready as ever I will be
for America, or I will be ready once I
get myself a hat, it being winter and all.
I walk stiff-legged toward Christopher St.,
see too many blocks between 10th and 11th,
and find that the city is skewed, sweetly,
for those who see the skyline or bridge
in this poem's wavy right-hand margin.
My regenerate heart pumps like a bird,
floating on auto, ever unwilling to land.

AFLOAT, THE IMMIGRANT MARTYR ELECT

I step off the plane,
bob like flotsam
above the scene
of future martyrdom.

The world machine
—*I know*—waits to greet me
with blood tests, green
ink, spy cameras, ID.

Nobody is there. I
do not understand.
I know how to fly,
not how to land.

In Quetta, Queens,
and West Asia, PA,
I found my cousins.
They shouted all day,

wept together at night.
Weekends spent
in study, we ate
only halal and lent-

ils. For weeks on end
I heard no word
of English spoken
but 'New York!'

Light falls, stars drown.
Grief rises, wearing feathers.
In this way we are one,
we die together.

IT WASN'T UNTIL THE LAWYER
TOLD ME I

could not leave that it got to me. I was
struck so deep by the notion of home
lost, I could barely breathe or sleep or dream.
I'd come out of the subway in one of those
Manhattan canyons and for a moment see
the stretch of street between Sree Liquors
and the left turn to the sea where a Russian
freighter ran aground in suburban Bombay.
The lawyer said I'd let things drift so far
that now I'd have to pay the price, she said,
berating me. All I could do was agree,
for I had let everything drift as I stepped
through my new life, dozy on downers
and meds. I thought of the life I left behind
and it seemed like some sort of blessing
suddenly, everything I tried so hard to escape.
I remembered waking every morning, nothing
on my mind but the tick of the lampman's
needle on the stem, telling me to suck
quickly at the pipe, before the pellet burned.
The sick-sweet grace of opium, like love
enveloping me, as the unhurried orange light
lit up the room in the late afternoon and I
picked up my books, my change, my shoes,
took a bus to the city where my wife waited
to feed me, the day's mail and newspapers folded

by my plate, as if I'd been working hard all day,
and the lawyer on the phone from Miami said
I'd waited too long, the price would be steep,
and I said yes, it is steep, the price, steep indeed.

THE MAN WHO MARRIED WATER

lived alone with his love,
together they churned or quiet
lay. His wife and he,
solitaries, rode the river to the
sea. Every tributary
led to her, to water.
Though his wife be jealousy,
she was water, she watched with
eyes of rain as the whales'
ancient terrain cracked,
the old routes now
led elsewhere, to a great
head stunned by land,
bound by sand. He
found himself and drowned.

The man who married fire
married everything.
He married desire,
filled the room
with his striving.
(He *was* consumed.)

The man
     who married
          air, saw

himself fall
    into a spiral,
        his hands

gripped tight
    on the wheel
        of a plane

hurtling
    down, a
        plane that

was
    not
        there.

Only he who married
earth was unsurprised.

SEPTEMBER 10, 2001

How much harder it is to speak
when I have spent the whole day silent.
I would like to stop someone,
leave my room in the evening and stop
someone, a man without hope,
or a woman bent double, as if she were
searching the sidewalk for gems caught in
the cracks, and I would tell her that each
of us walks with the same impossible burden,
knowing that only the stars will last—
she will listen to me, hear what I say,
and go on her way, bent over as before,
never looking up at the approaching sky.

II

SHAPESHIFTER

HOW TO BE A GIRL

Tiny cherubs of joy paddle the air.
Must I mention their preposterous wings?
No: I sit. I pull the door shut,
the cubicle expands like feathers.

The girl walks in, hesitates.
I watch her stop her shoes next door,
the bottoms of her frayed blue jeans.
(I'm trying not to make a sound.)

She bends down, places paper
on the seat, carefully sits.
I watch the shoes face forward,
the jeans fall to her feet.

I listen, then, to the sound
of fabric falling, down
to the floor of the stall.
The girl is gone.

I pull on her things—
shoes, underwear, jeans. Again,
the sound of God's snake hissing:
sudden swell of breasts on my chest.

Outwards I soften.
Stubble falls from my face.

19

A cleft of African violet
swells with the sea.

My lifeline lengthens.
My seat fills out.
I feel my smell change—spicy,
mysterious, so sweet I gag for fear.

HOW TO BE A TOAD

Take three fresh spores
with a dram of rum,
hold it on your tongue

for longish moments.
Pack all thoughts of gold
in a small leather case

the size of a sapphire.
Say to yourself repeatedly,
"I'll never again be beautiful."

HOW TO BE A LEAF

Hold your breath until
you are God's green thoughts.
Stop eating,

air will suffice for food.
Water is another matter:
the skin absorbs moisture,

eyes adjust,
limbs grow inward.
Conjugate patience.

Worship women and trees.

HOW TO BE A HORSE

Know the nostril,
all power gathers there.
Inflate yours until the blood sings.

You will need all your training
to be horse, not ass.
It is a thin crossing

perilous to the absent-minded
and the estranged of heart.
Avoid all latitudes.

HOW TO BE A CROW

Learn to name the animals
—Stinking, Babbling, Breedy,
Querulous, Maddened, Jet.

Usurp the duties of God.
Why not?
This is what poets do.

As for crow,
kill colour,
turn black.

24

HOW TO BE A BANDICOOT

Assume dominance
over the underworld.
Your enemies are legion

—eat them.
Eat everything.
You must build your strength,

change will surely come.
Your eyes are red legends.
Your name is Adam.

HOW TO BE A KRAIT

This one is easy,
let your grief take over.
Enjoy salt.

Forget the rest.
When your skin falls off,
sere as bone,

laugh out loud.
That is the first thing. The second:
Avoid the mongoose.

III

ACHE

FOOL AND FLEA

Dearly beloved
we are gathered here
to join together
this fool and this flea
in holy matrimony.

Fool will sing,
flea will suck.
Fool will work,
flea will pluck.
Both will learn

the virtue of obedience.
Fool will give up his freedom.
Flea will give up
whatever chance
she may have had

at happiness.
Both will die.
Fool first.
Flea so full
she'll burst.

THE AIR THERE IS CROWDED

I

Here we stand, steps away
from our first home.
Look closely at the way

the picture takes shape: three rooms,
two faces, a patch of lawn.
We are smiling. You will cram

the house with red Kohima rugs,
Jaipur cotton, scrolled iron,
a rocking chair, greenery, jazz:

your signature in the corner
of each shining
room. Look again: I trace your

face in the ransacked air,
trawl the hall for a sign
that once I lived here not alone.

II

He stands by the bed where lately they lay
an instant, strangers joined by name.
The morning rush hushed now and still,
an absence too vast for thought to fill.

He stops to stare at a space on the wall,
remembers nothing but farewell too soon.
Idly swung, the cradle swings still.
Wondering, he roams from room to room.

The Post-its are tales too tall to tell,
the kitchen ghosts mostly want out.
What was it brought on this rout?
He takes a last look around: all's well.

BOTERO'S PEAR

A painted pear hangs by her bed,
too-ripe belly flesh I knead.
My job's to cleave like rock
to the bruises of her back.

She stares at her Botero pear,
each blemish glowing with flavour.
A red worm wriggles the skin, and I
wriggle too, blind in my turn, supine.

The blue hour stills my hand and breath,
frees my brain past pain's last fever,
to the time of the fallen, *la ora de la ora,*
this hour and the hour of our death.

An egg of pear-shaped disclosure
fills my mouth, in a Bowery room,
with the one aphasic word
left at last to Baudelaire—*Crenom!*

VILLANELLE WITH A LINE FROM BAUDELAIRE

Obsidian his eyes in the neon light,
blinded by vision—a car, her hair.
Listen, love, how soft walks the night

in silver anklets, how timely the right
it grants us: to make ourselves better.
Obsidian his eyes in the neon light.

Driving away, her wires pulled tight,
she watches him fade from her mirror.
She'll walk, and listen to the night.

How well he talked, blazing with insight.
How did his fervour not convince her?
Obsidian his eyes in the neon light.

Ungainly, unkempt, a dodo in flight,
he finds himself saying, I am truer.
Listen, his love loves the night.

And he? Calmer, it takes all his might
to shamble on as love's lost lover.
Obsidian his eyes in the neon light.
Listen, love, how soft walks the night.

THERE'S A CHINESE WALL
BETWEEN US

Smoke seep, tire hiss,
motor roar—
a din that does not cease.

Next door, a dour
man, ardent
in dark glasses, snores,

a glottal stop and start.
I wait for
you to climb out

of the slumber
that divides
us. You shudder,

slip into the tide;
your hair
upswept as you ride.

Your feet syncopate their
sleepwalk
rhythms. Your bare

hands pare dreams, invoke
breasts;
your thighs unlock.

I watch your hands at rest,
blind
baby animals in aspect.

How small they seem
in flight
from the giant in your dream.

SAILOR'S LOG

Tacked to the dark
swell of her back,

I wake up dreaming.
Morning

spills like milk
across the floor. Birds build

fractured arpeggios;
my friends in chaos.

They speak
the secret words I work to keep

safe in my chest.
Why say the rest?

I long to be
misery,

my race obscure in a crowded sea,
shipwrecked, dizzy,

free.

PSALM SECULAR

When you I taste
god awakes
from a century's
sleep or murder.
I fold my hands,
press your blessings
to my head.

I kneel abed,
mouth small praises
where thy thighs
collide. I bow, arise.
Soon the sun
will do the same,
arise and bow.

I take two pears
from the Gauguin bowl,
shine them with your slip.
We eat sweet and fast.
Juice flecks our lips.
"Gravid!" I shout,
for the poor joy of it.

And you? Laughing,
my name in your eyes,
you cry one word.

The moon that hangs
above the street
on a silver thread
lifts its skirt to dance.

IV

THE GENESIS GODOWN

For every word has its marrow in the English
tongue for order and for delight.
Christopher Smart, 'Jubilate Agno'

ENGLISH

Here I stand for the seventh and last time,
by a sign that says, 'Welcome to Bombay.'
It could be any great city—crammed,
brimming with rage and suffrage—
I would be ruined still by syntax, the risk
and worry of word committed to stone.
English fills my right hand, silence my left.

Walking to the *dabbawallah*'s shop
for a copper wrist bone to replace the one
I wore out, I hum with knowledge
stretched as far as it can go and further,
to give you now seven plums
that range across the seven colours
of wisdom, each with its own worm, each
called by its own loving name: Alias,

Stretch, Gall, Fear, Blister, Scrum, Mankind.
Ripe with history, they bristle with residual
martial vigour and the sounds of battle,
not your familiar figures of good and evil
but players on a grimmer no-man's land
between experience lived and written:
you are etched in water, sculpted in wind
unless remade by the transfiguring hand.

All else is vanity and play, death-before-
and death-after-life. So pick your worm

carefully, look for flavour and vitality,
place in a full-bore metal thimble and
drop into ear or mouth. Ignore pain,
all discomfort is momentary,
possibly false. Move on to the kingdom
displayed before you. If you want the dung

beetle, you must take all six—rampant
males (one dead of a sensualist's disease)—
and place them near your navel, where
they like to meet. As for me, by the city's
north walls, near the ladies' latrine,
I set a flotilla of baby striders
afloat on the sticky green water.

I fill my hat, take with me as many
as I can. Their joyous humming lifts
us aloft, airborne like our brothers,
the giant flying beetles of my home.
Smearing honey on my skin, I let them
drink me to their fill. They are alive
and well; they deserve to be happy.

After all, this is where I live, a place
they too have chosen.
I see them now waiting for a gesture. I
raise my fist and provide. I see my winged,
scaled, armoured siblings slap their genitals
once more with rage and decry the terrible
litanies of St. Thomas, *"Mary, you too may
become a living spirit resembling males.*

For every woman who makes herself male
will enter the Kingdom of Heaven." I take
the female dung beetle by her tiny hand
and follow Her Daintiness into the best room.
She is too awed to speak, too cowed to say
thank you, but she will lead us, I know,
fearless in God's crazy teeming gardens.

SUMMER

Colour the hornèd snail
red for the fire that begets it, keep it
safe from the sun that robs it,
colour its home white on white
(make it rich enough to fill in
for the absence of shade trees,
conversation, or hope for comfort),
fold the light above it, and stand
beside your emissaries,
the Saguaro, the Joshua, the sea
without end, or pity, or water,
until something clicks inside us like light;
we are here to sing the permanent
cadence of sand, here am I, ready.

MOON

Arched and pitched to light tight as a talking drum,
I move nocturnal systems of poverty and frenzy,
my single stare lets lovers share the sweet span of hands,
my Dionysian currents, purple in subordinate air,
fill this miser's ward with silver coins of plenty;
I am Anarch, mistress and master of great Stonehenge,
flocks of firefly bearers hum the midnight's song
in tongues unknown to babbling man, Babylon, Babel:
call me by my name, though my name's a braid,
my name is moon, *it is not*, I am moon, *I am not*,
my sly eye's wanton twin is fat, white, everywhere;
I am turned by water, returned by the crescent,
quartered and corrected by the many-maned ocean—
when you stumble home on unlit roads and fields
of burnt-out resin, the nod-poppies of oblivion,
fix your eyes upon my spilt wide-open single one,
know that above you, always above, I wait to speak
of star or wave—*what else?*—the red robes of birth,
the passing craze of infancy; answer me no answer,
no one say no thing, let word be light be Cyclops,
I am your place in the comfort-making hearth,
cell of bone and runic parchment, papyrus pap
and driftwood, a last dance of twilight before
the trumpets shrill, I am your sister, your mother
moon am I, confidante of couches robed in analytic
cloth, bedlamite, friend to traitor and debauch,
whore of god, condoled by hellion and monarch,
I am this I am, moon-made, remade, maker of moon.

MONSOON

Oyster-tongue, mangrove maw, the river's raw
sour breath, its moist air encumbered with mud,
mad with waiting and grief, ready now to shed
upwards its uncoiling of earth's dry dirt-thirst,
long-held summer vertigoes of the ringing light
when the safe-sided contours of Kerala blur
to dazed stillness before the grand chaos of wind,
every fur and scurry must stop, pause in a pose of praises
    and prayer;
then in the small rain something fierce stirs
the river's grim, single-minded currents, furrowed
by history's keel, trawled by the spinning sleepers
fallen to its revolving arms—even the changeful
river knows this change will turn vast systems
awry—and the true rain begins: random power
endowed with shower of bounty, whips wind,
shreds vine, cracks bark, mangosteen, jackfruit,
slaps the baby palm, uproots lemon, tapioca,
flattens the cowering tufts of pineapple, and douses
the world in torrents of self-cycled water, maddened
by sea-rhythm and pounding heartless drudge
for unclocked hours, a constant torment of deluge
slow on the green land, the river, the annihilated air
—snakeholes flooded, monkey and woodpecker
mute, cats made fearful, cattle clustered—
the houses that funnel a rush of worried water,
water plumes through its own wet world, fierce

in its dream of water, and water made flesh of water,
a perfect craze of water, the mother of water,
of water creatures born from the water in this line.

DAWN

Surrounded by revellers of starlight and sea-scrum,
our green-grown house fits snug inside the music,
its trance-sparked triple-headed serpents,
phosphorescent sea monsters on shore to dance
and regard the slowed time, motion stilled to a stop;
the hiss and slap of surf remain, all other sound
drowned, and always above us the absence of light,
the stilled air a mirror of our geologic need—
false dawn, still unseen, little more than a notion,
waved away as some collective hallucination—
then true brightness begins
to bleed across the sky a circumscribed swell of bass,
cryptic the beat of Eden's demoniac percussionist,
a pulse-strumming contrarian whose enjambments
thicken the air to a glowing bubble of firelight, who
drives the dawn to a prodigious flowering, counter-
points the crack of carrion crow's first call
and the bone engine of the day's new castanet;
when morning's swift machine overtakes the stars,
scatters around us the mercy of brightness,
this oracular dawn reveals us for what we are:
a heaving tribe of bodies blessed at the feast,
as if each were a bowstring plucked and left to ring
some signature tune, a new and tonic metronome
more varied than the multimodal juggling of the sea:
uncontrolled, speed-made, fearful, wide-eyed, weeping,
we grapple with the permanence of ecstasy and time,

our arms upraised in praise for love's racing anapests,
for this frenzied mythmaking, for the mystic-riven
morning's holy page of dawn, spoken in a song.

WINTER

Waking in white light I stepped out of the house
you share with husband and child, left you sleeping,
the House of Unnamed Dread open above you—
stumbled past sequoia and oak, five hundred years
of gardening gathered toward a cold disclosure
half-understood in the apocryphal fall, its off-
season secret of sieved light waiting to be shared,
up where the delicate sister of air exhales a tune
so strange it appropriates every stir and spill,
the curved Haar of mind-made Doune—you wake
in the House of Grape to desolations of the dead;
morning's slow-moving secret, already spread,
intones monochrome inversion of tree-bole, stone,
approximates hue and tone, the tumult of sunlight,
irregular pulsings of soil and dew, depleted
by the absence of filigree, suspension of colour;
no birds, no leaves, no sunshine, November,
snuffed to distant knowledge of ash, gray on gray
in a blanked-out sky, so distracted by weather
it engenders nothing, believes, invokes even less,
the half-hearted promise nulled by a purifying
storm of impacted measure, tight as I hug my coat,
close to a conclusion, knowing now how it will be,
the practised poise of winter, its insistent soothing
and precision, an Omega of northern estrangement
sealed into stone—*whose snow is this, billowing*
like linen?—so, I know and bless this ground,

the sodden seat where soon tomorrow you will sit,
unable to create a nostalgia of scent, or of me,
undone by the winter first told you on this page.

MY GRANDMOTHER'S FUNERAL

What stories you know, closed in the worm's dominion,
histories composed for the doomed enclosure of bone,
hair and fingernail fragment; the yellow hoops removed
from your ears and wrists. *I alone am left to tell this love.*
Light drowns in water, uncertain, unseen from this church,
whitewashed on a hill in the lush south. *I alone am left.*
The congregation stands entranced, white shirts and mundus
starched, sung aloft on ancient rhythms, the talismanic glow
of hymns repeated in a tongue all of us remember and nobody
understands. Some words promise an impossible redemption:
barachimo, deyvam, shudham, slomo. *My words are water.*
The patriarchs' evening censers pass the scent of smoke
from hand to hand, from end to end of a heaving sunlit room
where Syriac, the first figure of faith, waits with his fierce
accountings—your ally in the conundrums of Christ,
his mother, her red heart bared. *Here am I, empty of words.*
At dawn, in single beds, you and your husband lay chaste
in matrimony, a wedlock holy as hands, *I am made mute,*
perfected your children, the young dead become legend,
oversaw the strict enunciation of shekels, rice and prayer.
The slow erosions of memory, your tidy acres overgrown,
ungentle stripping of faces, names, an ignoble disrobing
for the writer you were, grace, the first of our long line.
Crawling to eternity, alone in the one house so many sons
and daughters embarked from, *left alone to die,* you faced
the curse of longevity placed on the women of our tribe
with a wilful retrieval of dignity: the clenched refusals

of food and water, a final naysaying to the sanctification
of all who lived to your great age: a life-affirming *No!*
that resounds now through the walls, fallen, of your house.

V

ACHE

THE OTHER THING

The other thing I want to tell you
about my grandmother is how un-
interested she was in cooking and
how powerless she felt finally
about all that chastity. She wanted
life, but the food on her table
was always the same. She told of
Sundays past, the laughing season,
she, a wife of promise, lost.
As the magistrate's bride
in a small coastal town, she took
a turn away from the feast,
to end up hungry and alone.
At the end, she found
her way to glory: she said
water was too sweet,
chocolate too spicy, it brought
tears to her eyes, nothing was right,
not salt, not bread, nothing
helped, so she stopped food. She
stopped.

MEANWHILE, OVER IN ORISSA

Sometimes I see clearly, like a man
recovering from long illness.
On this ash-gray Ash Wednesday
I try to take coffee or stand
but little things trip me up:
my face in the kitchen mirror,
a grainy image folded on the bed,
an Indian rooster's insane crowing.

Daylight is worse by far. I see
my brain's clenched fist
command the body to rise.
I stop and cannot breathe.
The book's blurred runes flap
their wings, and pyramids of gods
lift red hands, their mouths
stained with a kind of love.

What can be said about the night?
Why point out its colour and smell?
Or the Australian missionary
and his two small sons
who pray in a burning jeep.
Saffron men dance around them,
their ash-lined foreheads
tremble like crosses in the heat.

i.m. Graham Staines

THE BROWN NUDE

On your chest, a sebaceous rose,
its mystic pose enhanced
by your prayerful painter's hands,

whose anointing spirals
colour the air. Crow
crawls across your eyes,

caws the evening
litany, insane.
We drop red rum,

past the blackened treetops.
In the room behind us
perspective tilts,

veers to places askew.
The brown nude stands tall,
nutbrown boy-breasts

agleam in the oiled light;
a young Tiresias,
or buff *ardhnareshwar*,

her wisdom won hard
from quarrels
with herself.

for Akbar Padamsee

THE BOREDOM ARTIST

Life, said Hobbes, is nasty, brutish, and short.
He left out boring, as grim a condition as any.
His tigerish namesake's epiphany,
in 20-point captions, is a Sunday slot.
Then there's Chekhov, who, a moment ago, wrote,

The earth is beautiful, as are all God's creatures,
only one thing is not beautiful, and that is us.
Between philosopher, toy tiger, doctor, there's
a ladder of land no man claims as his.
I'll settle down there with old friends, familiars:

a monkey, my famous barking birds in pairs,
and defrocked Sukhvinder, the bald brahmin bear.
Dawn, like whiskey, half-lights a watery world:
all things break down to flesh, food and fear.
It's late December in Fleetwood, downstate NY,

"glorious showers, thunderclouds continue".
My mind unwinds as the century slows,
dribbles its years to a whining close,
and defunct days peddle the news.
Listen: nothing, not even love, is true.

PORTRAIT OF THE ARTIST AS AN OLD GOD

A man of 63, on his back
in a rented room,
stares at the ceiling

fan, which gently cores
his vision into slices.
The sea repeats one line

he pretends not to hear.
It is already dusk,
the hour of the bat.

His hands will soon
blur in the gloom.
He lies there wide

-eyed, waiting,

ELEGIAC

We shake hands; yours are paper.
You tell of desecrated cities.
In the inner temple, blood-
brimmed bowls tremble at each
blow. On fine stalks of fear
your eyes
walk among drowned paddies,
boy pilots, breakfast whiskey, flak.
Stories whir like flies,
only one remains untold:

how can death be not useless?
why stain the air with grief
of my own, when so much hope
persists? Priests and monkeys
chatter like static; they
sift the fine lines that halo
your head. Ash heaves
upward. Bones fall, fill
the river, fat its oiled banks.
Your good eye sees soot

stain the sky. You salute
our awkward leave-taking.
I tried, you say,
but not enough, take
my hands and hold them,
bless me as I bless you.

Your hands
are mine. We hold a cup of air.
I drink the word 'holy'—I pray
a way to pay it forward.

for Dom Moraes

HE DO THE HUSBAND

When I stuck him with the knife,
she it was who screamed
louder than a struck heif-
er. It was harder than it seemed
to see her as his wife,

and see myself half-blind
with jealousy, tied
in a double bind.
He lay down and died.
I said, Make up your mind!

But she was done
talking. She lunged
at me. I put her down
with the dirt and dung
of Babylontown.

Her scream
was loud in my ear.
I walked to my Taurus,
put it in gear,
took off to Cream

and the Hallelujah Chorus.

VI

SHAPESHIFTER

HEROINATION

The News—not *news*—at Nine's plenty odd:
two peacemaker warheads gone astray,
the UN building lost at sea.
Ted the evening anchor's on the nod,
taking nonstop dictation from God.

The newsroom's top brass is in rehab,
everybody else at a meeting.
The first order of business is a stab
at good cheer—dimsum to go, with Tsing-
tao and cognac—on the company tab.

Ted slurs his first question, and the next,
"What's your policy, Mr, uh, Prime,
re. distribution, storage, the perfect clime?"
The reply: "To echo my mostly vexed
predecessor, I encourage the sublime:

more people must just say whoa!"
But the PM's got a bad feeling,
a sort of kind of sense of doom foretold;
voices in his head stutter, *told you so!*,
the studio lights set him reeling.

Next—*Dear God not now!*—a narcotic
buzz breaks out like the Chinese flu.
The sportscaster's narcoleptic,

Oprah's sympathetic,
and the weathergirl's copped one too.

Here at home, dad makes the usual noise,
"Front me two bags till the morning, boys."
"Don't you trust him," Mom says,
"He's ripped you off before, he'll do it
again. Give it here, you know *I'm* good for it."

So many dilated pupils (and teachers),
twisted endorphins and pro-tease inhibitors,
the whole world's high except for me.
I alone do my job: maintain and be
the last refuge of sobriety.

THE UNAUTHORIZED AUTOBIOGRAPHY
OF RAIN

I spoke to you in many
continents, whispered
soft consonants. Why bother?

In Euro I trilled nightly
a friendly anti-rhythm,
unbound by time or rime.

What comfort this knowledge,
this old conversation?
The strip malls still call. (I let

benedictions fall on Yankee soil,
spoke—*a joke*—in tongues.)
"No English here," I said in Siam,

heard my own forgotten name
from sources unreliable.
Nothing prepared me for monsoon.

How *prepare* for the mindless
yowls of Indic children?
My rain, they said, as if in explanation.

Am not, I said, as if in reply.

OPHELIA

I touch myself.
I kiss you.
You see nothing.

My dreams turn:
barking Pierrots,
copulations mysterioso.

Last night a bird spoke...
*Look for the light,
it will come from the north.*

. . . lies.
I long for ooze,
frogspawn,

bright ring of algae
round my throat.

INVENTORY

Body remembers blood beating
    in the womb,
the proprietary touch of dream.

Body remembers the brutal
    midwife's hushed job,
a damp room near the river,

incisions painting the skin,
    colour stitched down,
the unsurprising resolution.

Body remembers body, yours
    on loan, breathlessness,
the unhappy ending fulfilled.

Body remembers spawn
    battling upriver,
swelling a belly to bursting,

recalls the loud death
    threats at dawn,
crosses burning, firesmoke.

Body remembers sacred details,
    light like rum
firing up a brass spittoon.

Body remembers twin embalmers
    singing a capella,
itself unworthy of worship,

on my knees in the big house.
    Remembers, the body,
a fat lady, end as beginning.

YET ANOTHER MOTHER POEM

Light careens
through my veins,
makes me whole.
I inhabit

uninhabitable days.
Small whips of rain
crack at my back,
make me holy.

Water and air
pump red squalls
of love or pain.
I fall

into your room
on my frayed flat heels,
pillbox hat flat,
hands of opium tincture.

My winter breath blows
small sacraments
of air. There,
then gone.

AT KABUL ZOO, THE LION

So this is fear: tracers flaring
above the pen, the fat thud

of bullets, and the bigger sound
of animals leaving our lives.

Sad-eyed, the widow elephant
saw a cluster of shells

explode her enclosure.
She screamed in narrowing circles.

Shrapnel stopped her and she dropped,
the first to fall.

Everything burned:
the tiger shrugged fire

off his shoulders.
The capuchins tried

to escape their burning tails.
The hyacinth macaws,

spoonbills and hoot owls,
flamingoes aflame…

Only the llamas stood dumb
in that madness, stupid

to the end. I envied their emptiness.
Blind in one eye,

my jaw in shreds, my mane
singed to a useless crop,

I'm still here.
I wait for these men

to come to me.

SLUMMING IN BOMBAY, BEELZEBUB

found himself at home. Finally, he
had a reason for lethargy.
Inert like everybody else, unable to work,
he blamed the humidity.
No use to say, 'But B,
that's what this city does, man, saps you,
leaves you spent like change,
separates the dudes from the ditties.'
He was having none of it,
and then the boss arrived, unexpected,
on a Sunday.
But the boss—*now what?*—had changed.
Hard as it was to believe,
she was kind-hearted, distracted, funny,
endearing even.
The day she came to take him home,
they were seen at the Hanging Gardens,
hand in hand, watching the dust bees
ride their favourite pollen machines.
It was Christmas Day, just after dawn,
the heat and humidity at peace
it seemed, and Beelzebub's boss serene.

VII

MOVEABLE

LAND'S END

Undermined by grace and the roaring line,
we lay ourselves open, across the cross the
seafarers climbed, past white church, tufted
wave, the endless roil of raw sea and rock.

Here Peter still teeters; not rock, not man
but Englishman, his word on water writ.
Land's end or faith's? That was your question.
Now answered, my friend, for us it's wit's end.

for Adil Jussawalla

PASHUPATINATH

At "most famous Kathmandu",
tradesmen's wives
talking shopping,

we walked past
marijuana fields
barbed neck-high

in the noon yoga;
delicate pulsings
breathing the feathers,

each ribbed leaf
the colour of
parrot skin.

A bull of beaten gold
balanced on balls
so large they dwarfed

the nesting crowds.
With hands full of money,
flowers and prayers,

our unruly lines
mobbed the priest
who slapped each supplicant

across the head,
the smaller the donation
the louder the slap.

The giant bull
sat serene,
without regard,

his gold made ordinary
in the tightening dust.

KOVALAM

Saffron sun over Kovalam,
slum waters agleam, telling me
how the dream finally ended:
the journey half done, we undone.

Ancestral moonlight on the tracks
took us in a rush to confess
our impossible pilgrimage.
At the station, a wayward cross.

After all that overflowing,
misery was a kind of peace.
I sat at the edge of a world,
at the end of a life, smoking

endless cork-tipped cigarettes.
The sun—fat, old, obscene—
dipped its rear into the bleak
water. Nearby, a girl's high cry.

IMAGINARY HOMECOMING

At river's edge
I cup my hands,
drink until I'm drunk,

the cool water
made sweeter
with knowledge.

This is the end
of wandering under
other skies,

the untrue north of exile.
How many camps
like this one?

Heat or cold,
or a promise of better;
we washed our thirst

with more thirst,
ready always
for weather.

Each day
brought its measure
of movement.

Cow-dung houses
abandoned, cook fires
doused, horses slaughtered.

So many rude tongues
become familiar,
we learned to keep

our own language
secret and true
to our ears.

The rank rubric
of memory,
our only constant,

and the women,
children,
exhaustion.

I let the water
wet my face, taste
sun on my tongue,

woodsmoke
from the houses
on the hill.

LONDON

The air is shut too tight, its
unoiled hinges resist use.
Every day I assay
new methods of entry,
nothing works
but a handful of pills.

The light is wrong;
slant intent
grown homicidal,
it tells us something
relevant about
responsibility,

something I do not want
to hear. It is difficult
enough to breathe,
and get this line just right.
My friends have given in to
the prevailing wind

of neglect. You can tell
by their shoes, stacked
against the brute
passage of time.
The rubber soles are coded:
these shoes will last

longer than us.
Then there's the night
sweats, the chill wind
come straight off the moon,
aiming at me
its Jabberwock garrulity.

You get no rest here,
nobody does.
Even the rain wants to talk
of insomnia or shopping,
which, it says repeatedly,
is better than sex.

The river arches its scaly back,
inviting kin from above,
the mirror-river in the sky,
to join the monochrome
festivity, the tedious
feast, the permanent fun.

Time now to move,
for the motion and ease
of movement, everything
moving without meaning
toward the water
where once we lived.

DOUNE

He stops,
stunned by sun;
too bright for any country
other than
his own blighted one.

No mist, no Haar
follows him with mute intent.
Wherever he goes,
the tropics go too.
Until one blear morning,

laid low in the highlands,
he wakes in a child's room
guarded by tiny animals
—a monkey with a tail
long as a length of string,

a giraffe, seven bears,
droop-eared puppies—
and a multi-coloured ball of wool;
he wakes, I say, with fragments
from the memory museum,

unable to recall who he is,
or where he may be.
He keeps his eyes tightly closed,

hoping to hold on
to this pleasing amnesia;

he cannot remember
when last he felt so cheerful.
When he steps into morning,
there's a chill mist
thin as strands of cotton:

blank, absent, without meaning,
a landscape untouched
by history or memory,
a place whose weather
matches his own.

HONGKONG, 1997

What's he doing on this creaking barge,
tethered to a wintry island sea? What
does he hope to find, huddled under
wet tarpaulin? Unseen objects knock
against the hull. He's pared it down—all
of it—to this unlikely cohesion
of metal and wood, afloat on a whim
of candlelight, the moon clanging on water.
My God thou hast shriven me, he says
aloud. *Yes, Lord, thou hast taken from me*
all vanity and surcease. Bone-weary,
I beg recompense. I wait to be plucked
and played but all night thy terrible hands
push against the stern. Morning brings no
clarity but a pasty haze like the moon's,
though colder. Nothing's certain in this
kind of light. The old woman who rows him
to shore wears a veiled umbrella hat. Her
wide and unforgiving face is as impassive
as December on the salt South China Sea.

INDEX OF FIRST LINES

91

HAMISH HAMILTON

APOCALYPSO

Jeet Thayil was born into a Syrian Christian family in Kerala. As a boy he travelled through much of the Indian subcontinent and Southeast Asia with his father, T.J.S. George, a writer and editor. He worked as a journalist for twenty-one years in Bombay, Bangalore, Hong Kong and New York City. In 2005 he began to write fiction. The first instalment of his Bombay Trilogy, *Narcopolis*, was shortlisted for the Booker Prize and became an unlikely bestseller. His book of poems *These Errors Are Correct* won the Sahitya Akademi Award (India's National Academy of Letters), and his musical collaborations include the opera *Babur in London*. His essays, poetry and short fiction have appeared in the *New York Review of Books*, *Granta*, *TLS*, *Esquire*, *The London Magazine*, *The Guardian* and *The Paris Review*, among other venues. Jeet Thayil is the editor of *The Penguin Book of Indian Poets*.

ALSO BY JEET THAYIL

FICTION
Names of the Women
Low
The Book of Chocolate Saints
Narcopolis

POETRY
Collected Poems
These Errors are Correct
English
Gemini (two-poet volume with Vijay Nambisan)

AS EDITOR
The Penguin Book of Indian Poets
The Bloodaxe Book of Contemporary Indian Poets
Divided Time: India and the End of Diaspora

LIBRETTI
Babur in London
Talk is Cheap